BEAUTY FROM ASHES

A Wellness Journal

Tara Lee

ISBN (Paperback): 979-8-9878693-3-8
ISBN (Hardcover): 979-8-9872203-2-0
ISBN (eBook): 979-8-9872203-3-7

ACKNOWLEDGMENTS

To my firstborn son, Conrad Lile: You made me a mom. You filled my heart with such pride and joy. You had the most undeniable spirit. I still hear your beautiful laughter—it plays over and over in my ears. Your insane sense of self and your refusal to conform to ways of this world, I always admired. Your shocking sense of humor and extraordinary intelligence were God-given gifts. May God keep you in His arms as we keep you in our hearts, until we see you again.

> I will search for the rest of my life
> for moments filled with you.
> ~ Anonymous

To my son, Carter: You amaze me every day with your kind heart and quick wit. You have the most chill attitude of anyone I know. You do not let things of this life upset you or get you down, which is an amazing life skill I wish I had. I know you will use your gifts from God for good. God has great plans for your life. I am so extremely proud and grateful to have you as my son.

To my daughter, Tatum: You inspire me! You have such a great passion for life. You are fiery, kind and as beautiful on the inside as you are on the outside. You are the most loving and caring daughter I could ever ask for. I am so glad that you know Jesus and His great love for you. I love you to the moon and back.

My Story

In an instant, my life went from vibrant, full color to completely pitch-black. It was the moment that my oldest son, Conrad, took his own life. There is absolutely nothing that could have prepared me for a catastrophic loss of this magnitude. My beautiful son, Conrad, my strong, handsome, funny Marine taken in one instant.

I could hardly comprehend the words being spoken to me by the police officers that were standing on our driveway. They came to our home to give our family this life shattering news. I just remember screaming. "No, Dear God, no, noooooo God, please, no," pleading and begging with God, "Please God, please this cannot be true."

It is truly the worst kind of pain that I have ever known. It felt as if my heart was physically being ripped from my chest. I know that I was almost hysterical. I went directly into complete and utter shock, so as not to feel the full impact of this kind of pain all at once. I took the small bag of his personal belongings. I clung to it as tightly as I could, knowing this was all I had.

My two young children, Carter and Tatum were inside our home. I had to find a way to compose myself enough to walk in and explain to my two young children that Conrad, their brother, had just passed away.

CONRAD

My beautiful son – he had as much curiosity and joy as a child could hold. He filled my life and my heart completely with adoration and pride. His quick wit made us laugh hysterically; his beautiful eyes and half-smile could light up a room. I always felt as if he were an old soul, wise beyond his years.

As a child, he was content, silly, and ridiculously smart. Conrad was so much fun to watch grow-up. He was the sweetest, most content baby I have ever known and the funniest, happiest, and most likeable kid.

As he grew into his teenage years, he went from a super happy kid to an angry teenager, anger that I felt was coming from the absence of his biological father. This absence caused such immense deep pain, but not knowing what to do with this pain, it was displaced with anger and rebellion. I felt he tried to distance himself from me, trying to guard his heart from further disappointment and pain. I was the closest person to him, and he knew no matter what that I would love him unconditionally, so at times his anger was directed at me. This was especially tough for our family, since his younger brother, Carter, was just an infant at the time. As a mother, your instinct is to try to do anything and everything to help your child, so I did that. I started Conrad in counseling at the young age of 13. I spent countless hours reading books and searching for answers. Why couldn't my sweet boy just stay out of trouble? Why was my extremely smart boy doing so poorly in school? There was one question, I kept asking over and over. Why was it so hard for him to receive the unconditional love I had for him? Through the tough teenage years, I just wish I had some insight about what it means to live with depression. Conrad had a genetic predisposition on his father's side that included depression and addiction. I remember asking one counselor, "Do you think Conrad is depressed?" I did not even know the full extent of what that really meant. My complete ignorance in this area was overwhelming and in hindsight, it was painfully lacking. I thought that being depressed meant feeling sad from time to time, not knowing the demons that haunted him and the constant battle his mind was fighting. I was not equipped and felt I was failing my son. The well-meaning counselors stumbled to help Conrad as he usually told them what they wanted to hear. He was very smart, and this meant less time talking to a stranger about his problems. At his young age, he struggled to find the value in counseling.

So, my handsome young boy turned into a young man. Following high school, he enlisted in the

United States Marines. My heart filled with pride and fear, all at the same time. Our family traveled to San Diego to see him graduate after his grueling ninety-one days of Marine Corps boot camp. We could not believe the transformation. We were amazed by Conrad's discipline and the new young recruit that he had become. He loved the "Marines" and his new band of brothers.

Conrad spent the next few years in the service of our country and was deployed for two tours in Afghanistan. The years went by slowly. I was completely overjoyed when Conrad would get to call via satellite phone or have leave to come visit us. Our family was even lucky enough to go to North Carolina a couple of times to be with him after his deployment.

When he returned from his deployment in Afghanistan, things changed. He met a girl, whom he told me he loved and they eventually married. My heart was full once again, seeing Conrad the happiest he had been in years. I opened our home and welcomed our son's wife to our family. But just after their first year of marriage, signs of distress started to show. Conrad did his best to put on the good face of a happy couple, keeping me in the dark as to the severity of what was really going on. To my complete dismay, shock, and disappointment, Conrad's wife left him. He had put all of his love and trust in her. He believed that she loved him. She left him broken beyond repair. The abandonment he felt from his father and now the one person whom he finally opened up to and trusted his heart with broke it into a million pieces. It was just more than what he could take. On August 29, 2012, Conrad lost his battle with depression and made the choice to end his own life.

It Starts Here

The purpose of this wellness journal is to get you started on a path to healing. The trauma of great loss can be felt for months and years to come. Grief is a personal journey. At many times it may feel like it is a journey of survival. Grief is as individual as a snowflake. There are no two people that grieve the same. Grief is not linear, it does not continue in a straight line; grief ebbs and flows like the ocean. Some days are calm, whereas some days are so turbulent that you feel as if you are drowning. Some days you may feel as if you are doing much better, only to have a single thought, a single song, or a single memory bring you into a pool of tears and agony.

Although I wish that you were not on this journey, you can take comfort in knowing that others who have been on this path have learned to navigate, grow, become stronger, be more compassionate, and even reach back and help others to do the same. That is the purpose of this journal, and it is my personal prayer for you.

This journal is a way to write down the heaviness of your heart. My hope is that you become lighter as your feelings and thoughts spill onto these pages. In the early stages of my grief, a sweet friend of mine, Deborah, gave me a journal. It was gorgeous, covered with flowers and bound with colorful ribbon. I did not know at the time this journal would become such huge part of my healing journey. On those pages, I placed my broken heart and anguished soul. I have now been journaling for over ten years.

In the early months, I could not see myself making any forward progress.

I felt as if I was just trying to get through one hour and then just trying to make it through one day. My early entries are extremely difficult, filled with the pain of guilt and sorrow and the feelings of being alone in my pain. The tear-stained pages remind me of the darkest, longest, and hardest days of my life. I have read many times that grief is a passage and not a place to stay. I definitely did not want to and could not stay in that place.

There is a simple goal: find what helps you get into a better place and make that choice everyday: to live beautifully broken.

Grief Work

> The only way around is through.
> ~ Robert Frost

This one is tough. Grief work is allowing yourself to feel all the feelings that you feel.

(Wow! That is a lot of "F" words.) Cry! Let it out; cry until you have no more tears. If you feel like screaming, do that. Scream into a pillow, or scream out loud. If you feel like punching or kicking something, take a kickboxing class.

Part of my grief work was having conversations with my son, Conrad. I spent a lot of time in my backyard before anyone was awake. I just poured out my broken heart. I talked to him and told him how much I loved and missed him. I let him know how much I was hurting. I told him all the things that I felt were left unsaid. I also used this time to deepen my relationship with God. There have been thousands of conversations with God asking to give me the strength to just keep moving forward and give me the ability to still be a good mom, friend and daughter.

If you don't allow yourself to feel every feeling, chances are that you will bottle them up, and the overwhelming emotions may come out sideways later as displaced anger, emotional breakdowns or anxiety. I, unfortunately, have gone through all, at one time or another.

My amazing counselor, Dr. Debra, often told me grief work is hard and you may feel exhausted, like you just ran a marathon. Unfortunately, this marathon this marathon does not come with a shiny medal at the end. It comes with a small but simple thank you to God that I made it through one more day.

Prayer and the Word of God

The power of prayer: On one of my toughest days, I vividly remember asking God to just take me; the pain I felt was excruciating, unbearable, and unceasing. I did not want to go on. I remember thinking this is what Conrad must have been feeling before he decided to end his own life, such deep, immense pain, hopelessness, brokenness, and suffering. I know God heard my prayer, but thankfully, God did not answer that prayer. There are still days today that knock me to my knees, literally! It is on those days I stay there and give my heart to God. I may not understand God's plan. I will walk by faith. I will not lean on my own understanding but God's promises and His word for strength, comfort, direction, and healing. There are verses all through the Bible that talk about being broken:

The Lord is close to the brokenhearted and saves those who are crushed in spirit. (Psalm 34:18)

My soul weeps because of grief; strengthen me according to your word. (Psalm 119:28)

God blesses those who mourn, for they will be comforted. (Matthew 5:4)

All praise to God and Father of our Lord Jesus Christ. He is the source of every mercy and the God who comforts us. He comforts us in all our troubles so that we can comfort others. When others are troubled, we will be able to give them the same comfort God has given us. (2 Corinthians 1:3-5)

Cast your cares on the Lord and he will sustain you; he will never let the righteous be shaken. (Psalm 55:22)

EXERCISE

> *Exercise not only changes your body, it changes your mind, attitude and mood.*
>
> ~ Anonymous

They say that exercise is the most underused antidepressant that there is. Use it! Take a yoga class, go for a bike ride, run, dance, walk, hike, lift weights, swim, or take a barre class. There were many days while doing yoga that at the end of class, there is a still pose called the Savasana. I would lay there silently with tears streaming down my face. The overwhelming emotions that were building came pouring out. Yoga is a great healer; it is good for your emotional and physical health.

I also set a goal to run the Phoenix Marathon in under 4 hours. I spent months training. In those months, I spent a lot of hours just running by myself. On those runs, I would use that time to talk to God, pour out my brokenness to Him, and ask for strength and guidance. I dedicated my race to Conrad. While I was running, I saw a young man in my path wearing a Marine shirt. I felt that was a nod from Conrad cheering me on. I reached my goal, in a time of, 3 hours and 55 minutes.

There are days that you may not feel like doing any activity. Just do what you can, and give yourself grace on days that you can't.

COUNSELING

> *At times our own light goes out and is*
> *rekindled by a spark from another person.*
> *Each one of us has cause to think with*
> *deep gratitude of those who have lighted*
> *the flame within us.*
> *~ Albert Schweitzer*

There is so much to be said for a good counselor. This, also, is not an easy task. It may take several tries before you find a good fit, but keep trying. You have to feel like you can trust your counselor and feel that they are listening and make you feel completely comfortable. You want to feel like the counselor really understands what you are going through. The counselor should be giving you coping skills that help. There were times that my counselor, Dr. Deb, and I would cry together. I can never forget or repay her for the healing that I received through countless hours of me talking and her listening.

I reached out to a counselor for my children within a couple of weeks of their brother's passing, but it took several months before I was even ready to get myself the help of a counselor. It may take time before you feel like you need it. It may be that you have a big circle of friends and family that are your support system. You may reach out to them to lean on.

There are also so many options in the way of group support. For me, listening to others who have gone through a similar circumstance, knowing that they are further along in their grief journey, helped me to realize that that restoration is possible.

It is important to find out if it is something that works for you. I had one counselor at a Survivors of Suicide meeting tell me to try coming to meetings for at least a month before I decide if it was for me or not.

FRIENDS AND FAMILY

Hold tight to the friends that stay by your side; keep them forever because they are hard to come by. There will always be those who do not understand your journey or choose not to be near during this time. This is very painful and hard to understand, especially if it is someone you considered to be a close friend or family member. In going through devastating loss, you truly find out who your friends are.

One morning, in the beginning of my grief journey, one of my kind and compassionate friends, Sherry, placed coffee, some hand-picked flowers, and a card in my backyard. She knew this was the place that I came in the morning to sit and cry.

On another occasion, my sweet family sent our family the most thoughtful care package. Each one of my siblings and Conrad's cousins sent pictures, quotes, keepsakes, and handwritten letters about Conrad.

I also had my kindhearted and caring friends, Nancy and Stacie, just out of the blue, send me songs, Bible verses, and quotes that always lifted my spirit and reminded me that I was not alone in my walk. I will never forget and have such gratitude for the friends and family that stayed by my side and those who showed up and never left me during the hardest days of my life.

Goal Setting

Make a goal every day. This can be as simple as getting out of bed, eating healthy food for your body, going for a walk outside, spending some time with a friend, or listening to some uplifting music. If there is one thing that you can accomplish, do that. This will hopefully lead you to other things that you can do; start small and build from there.

After years of being a real estate agent, I decided that I wanted to go into the esthetics field. I set a goal to go back to school to accomplish this. I graduated from an esthetics school this past winter. I will use my gift of helping and nurturing people in my new career field.

Helping Others in Need

> And do not forget to do good and share with others, for such sacrifices God is pleased.
> ~ Hebrews 13:16

You never know what someone is going through, so a kind word, a smile, a listening ear, or a helping hand can mean so much. I believe that there is much to be gained by helping others. During the first few days after Conrad's passing, our sweet friends put a fridge on our porch, and each night meals were prepared and brought to us. Our friends' generosity and caring were so overwhelming, we felt so blessed during our time of need. Since that time, our family has, in turn, prepared meals for other families, in our church and in our neighborhood who are in need. We know firsthand how simple but how much it means to someone to have one less thing to think about while going through a tough time.

GRATITUDE

> Gratitude turns what we have into enough and more, it turns denial into acceptance, chaos into order, confusion into clarity, it makes sense of our past and brings peace for today and creates a vision for tomorrow.
> ~ Anonymous

This was a very hard thing for me for a very long time. Although I have a tremendous amount of wonderful people in my life, grief kept me from seeing all of the amazing things that were right in front of me. I always told my counselor that I felt so guilty being sad because I had so many great people in my life, but when I felt happy, I almost felt like it was a betrayal to my son. How could I be happy when Conrad was no longer with us? The small steps I took toward gratitude started simply by pinning gratitude quotes on my Pinterest board. I honestly think it was several years before I was even able to write in my gratitude journal again, but when I finally did, I was able to write down all of the beauty that I still have in my life. I had to search for new things to be grateful for. I have a renewed relationship with my savior Jesus Christ, learning to trust and lean in when things are the most difficult. I have a super funny and kindhearted son, Carter; and a super awesome daughter, Tatum, who is just about the kindest, caring and most beautiful girl ever.

Animals

> Some angels choose fur instead of wings.
> ~ Anonymous

The unconditional love of an animal can be very healing. We have a 10-year old Morkie (Maltese-Yorkie) named Bella. She is the sweetest, best dog! I cannot count the number of times that she has licked away my tears or just sat with me on my hard days. Animals, I believe, can sense if you are feeling sad; they meet you where you are and expect nothing in return (except maybe a belly rub). They are so loyal, and they are always happy to see you and love being with you.

LAUGHTER

Laughter is the sound of the soul dancing.
~ Jerod Kintz

Never underestimate the healing power of laughter. Grief takes so much from you. It even takes the smile from your face and the joy from your voice. Laughter was very difficult and did not come easily or at all in the early days. I just had to learn to allow myself to laugh again.

READ

There is something so comforting in reading about someone else's journey that can give peace and hope for your own journey. You somehow connect to the author when you go through something they describe. Right after we lost Conrad, I remember searching for answers – anything to help me navigate this unimaginable loss. I checked out six books from the library. I was in such a grief fog that I could only make it through a couple of paragraphs before realizing I didn't have the capacity to understand written words on a page. As time went on, I have read so many books on grief, inspiring books of triumph over tragedy. This also inspired me to share my own story.

FAKE IT
TILL YOU MAKE IT

> I say, "I'm fine, thanks",
> because I simply cannot describe the pain.
> ~ Anonymous

One word: fine. It is the word I used for over a year when someone asked how I was. Nothing could be further from the truth! I was not fine. I lost my son. I am not good at public grieving, somehow sparing everyone else feelings while burying mine. I got really good at crying myself to sleep, picking myself up off the floor, and crying in the shower to hide my tears. I had to find a way to make it through the day, praying that I wouldn't run into anyone at the grocery store or at the gym. I came across the "fake it till you make it" saying, praying that if I pretended long enough that I was okay, I would really be "okay."

MUSIC

> Music can heal the wounds that
> medicine cannot touch.
>
> ~ Anonymous

Music is so powerful! It can take you back to a time or place with just a few notes. I used music as a healer. There were days I would turn the music up as loud as it would go and just run – anything to drown out the sorrow. On other days, one of my Conrad songs would come on the radio as I got into the car, and I would just sob, driving down the freeway. If it was a better day, the song would make me smile because somehow I knew that it was Conrad giving me a "Hi, Ma. I'm thinking of you".

FORGIVENESS

> When you forgive, you in no way change
> the past, but you sure do change the future.
> ~ Bernard Meltzer

In order for one to heal completely….one must first forgive. I was at least four years into my grief journey when I felt there was a common theme that was playing over in several areas in my life. My pastor at church talked in great detail about forgiveness. He gave an example of forgiveness offered from one man to another man, who had accidentally killed that man's wife. I remember sitting in church, tears streaming down my face, thinking what a powerful example of forgiveness that was. Within the same week, my friend Aurelia – She is filled with the spirit of God – sent me several messages about true forgiveness and how I must ask God for His divine help. Then in the same week, by chance, I happened to rent the movie The Shack. The biggest piece of the movie was a timely and perfect message on forgiveness. I felt God was giving me the direction that I needed the most.

In my case, I had several people that I had to forgive. I had to forgive myself. This one was the hardest. I have always felt God has entrusted my children into my care. I love my firstborn son, Conrad, with all of my heart and soul. I would have taken Conrad's place that day if only it could have saved him. I had to forgive myself for what I did not know, the feelings of failing my child. The feelings of "if I only would have" has replayed in my head a million times, and I have cried a million tears thinking about what I could have done differently. I had to just let that all go.

I asked God for His help. I also had other people close to Conrad that I needed to forgive.

Forgiveness does not mean that you condone the actions or that you need to let that person back into your life, but it frees your heart from the binds of anger, hate, and bitterness. I prayed that night, pleading to God to let me forgive not only myself, but the others as well. With the gift of forgiveness, I felt a huge weight was lifted and the healing continue.

Armor Up

Stand your ground, putting on the belt
of truth and the body of armor of Gods
righteousness. For shoes, put on the peace
that comes from the good news so that you
will be fully prepared. In addition to all of
these, hold up the shield of faith to stop the
fiery arrows of the devil. Put on salvation
as your helmet and take the sword of the
spirit, which is the word of God.
~ Ephesians 6:14-17

The weight of deep grief makes you very vulnerable. The spiritual forces of evil are very real, and you may find yourself in a real struggle. The full armor of God will give you protection in this battle. Through the years, there have been so many times that I have felt God's presence at just the right time and in just the right place. The right person, the right song, the right Bible verse—I know this is God's protection and provision.

Find Your Purpose

I feel God moving in my life every day. I focus on what I have instead of what I do not. I choose to have gratitude and show gratitude to those around me. I focus on God's promises and God's purpose for my life. I pray that God uses my pain for good. I live with God's grace in my heart and feel beauty where once there were ashes.

Your Turn

It may be that something else that will give you healing and peace. Use this space to write your ideas down; you may be a writer, photographer, an artist, or a gardener. Ask yourself, what are you passionate about? Or, before your great loss, what gave you the most joy?

Ideas: _______________________________________

____

____

____

____

____

Journal

Date: _______________________________________

I'm grateful for: _______________________________
____

My goal for today is: ____________________________
____

What is on my heart today: _______________________
____
____
____
____
____
____
____
____
____

Journal

Date: _______________________________

I'm grateful for: _______________________________

____

My goal for today is: _______________________________

____

What is on my heart today: _______________________________

____

____

____

____

____

____

____

____

____

Journal

Date: _______________________________________

I'm grateful for: ____________________________
____

My goal for today is: ________________________
____

What is on my heart today: ___________________
____
____
____
____
____
____
____
____
____

Journal

Date: _______________________________________

I'm grateful for: _______________________________

____

My goal for today is: ___________________________

____

What is on my heart today: ______________________

____

____

____

____

____

____

____

____

____

Journal

Date: _______________________________________

I'm grateful for: _______________________________

____

My goal for today is: ___________________________

____

What is on my heart today: ______________________

____

____

____

____

____

____

____

____

____

Journal

Date: _______________________________________

I'm grateful for: _____________________________

____

My goal for today is: __________________________

____

What is on my heart today: _____________________

____

____

____

____

____

____

____

____

Journal

Date: _______________________________

I'm grateful for: _______________________________

____

My goal for today is: _______________________________

____

What is on my heart today: _______________________________

____

____

____

____

____

____

____

____

____

Journal

Date: ____

I'm grateful for: ____________________________________
____

My goal for today is: ________________________________
____

What is on my heart today: ___________________________
____
____
____
____
____
____
____
____

Journal

Date: _______________________________________

I'm grateful for: ___________________________

____

My goal for today is: ______________________

____

What is on my heart today: _________________

____

____

____

____

____

____

____

____

____

Journal

Date: _______________________________________

I'm grateful for: ___________________________

____

My goal for today is: _______________________

____

What is on my heart today: __________________

____

____

____

____

____

____

____

____

____

Journal

Date: _______________________________________

I'm grateful for: ______________________________

____

My goal for today is: __________________________

____

What is on my heart today: _____________________

____

____

____

____

____

____

____

____

Journal

Date: _______________________________________

I'm grateful for: ___________________________
____

My goal for today is: ______________________
____

What is on my heart today: _________________

____

____

____

____

____

____

____

____

Journal

Date: _______________________________________

I'm grateful for: _____________________________

____

My goal for today is: _________________________

____

What is on my heart today: ____________________

____

____

____

____

____

____

____

____

____

Journal

Date: _______________________________

I'm grateful for: _______________________
____

My goal for today is: ____________________
____

What is on my heart today: ________________
____
____
____
____
____
____
____
____
____

Journal

Date: _______________________________

I'm grateful for: ____________________
____

My goal for today is: ________________
____

What is on my heart today: ___________
____
____
____
____
____
____
____
____
____

Journal

Date: _______________________________________

I'm grateful for: _______________________________

____

My goal for today is: ___________________________

____

What is on my heart today: ______________________

____

____

____

____

____

____

____

____

Journal

Date: _______________________________________

I'm grateful for: _____________________________

____

My goal for today is: _________________________

____

What is on my heart today: ____________________

____

____

____

____

____

____

____

____

____

Journal

Date: ___________________________________

I'm grateful for: _______________________

____

My goal for today is: ___________________

____

What is on my heart today: _____________

____

____

____

____

____

____

____

____

Journal

Date: ___________________________________

I'm grateful for: _______________________

____

My goal for today is: ___________________

____

What is on my heart today: ______________

____

____

____

____

____

____

____

____

____

Journal

Date: _______________________________________

I'm grateful for: _____________________________

____

My goal for today is: _________________________

____

What is on my heart today: ____________________

____

____

____

____

____

____

____

____

____

Journal

Date: _______________________________________

I'm grateful for: _______________________________

____

My goal for today is: ____________________________

____

What is on my heart today: ________________________

____

____

____

____

____

____

____

____

Journal

Date: _______________________________

I'm grateful for: _______________________________

____

My goal for today is: _______________________________

____

What is on my heart today: _______________________________

____

____

____

____

____

____

____

____

____

Journal

Date: _______________________________

I'm grateful for: _____________________

____

My goal for today is: __________________

____

What is on my heart today: _____________

____

____

____

____

____

____

____

____

Journal

Date: _______________________________

I'm grateful for: _____________________

____

My goal for today is: _________________

____

What is on my heart today: ____________

____

____

____

____

____

____

____

____

____

Journal

Date: _______________________________________

I'm grateful for: _____________________________

____

My goal for today is: _________________________

____

What is on my heart today: ____________________

____

____

____

____

____

____

____

____

____

Journal

Date: _______________________________________

I'm grateful for: _______________________________
____

My goal for today is: ____________________________
____

What is on my heart today: _______________________
____
____
____
____
____
____
____
____
____

Journal

Date: ___________________________________

I'm grateful for: ___________________________
____

My goal for today is: _______________________
____

What is on my heart today: ___________________
____
____
____
____
____
____
____
____
____
____

Journal

Date: ____

I'm grateful for: ____________________________________

____

My goal for today is: ________________________________

____

What is on my heart today: __________________________

____

____

____

____

____

____

____

____

Journal

Date: ____

I'm grateful for: ____________________________________

____

My goal for today is: ________________________________

____

What is on my heart today: ___________________________

____

____

____

____

____

____

____

____

____

Journal

Date: _______________________________________

I'm grateful for: _____________________________

____

My goal for today is: __________________________

____

What is on my heart today: _____________________

____

____

____

____

____

____

____

____

____

Journal

Date: ____

I'm grateful for: _____________________________________

____

My goal for today is: _________________________________

____

What is on my heart today: ____________________________

____

____

____

____

____

____

____

____

Journal

Date: _______________________________________

I'm grateful for: _______________________________
____

My goal for today is: _______________________
____

What is on my heart today: ___________________

____

____

____

____

____

____

____

____

____

Journal

Date: _______________________________________

I'm grateful for: _____________________________
____

My goal for today is: _________________________
____

What is on my heart today: ____________________
____
____
____
____
____
____
____
____
____

Journal

Date: ___________________________________

I'm grateful for: _________________________

____

My goal for today is: _____________________

____

What is on my heart today: ________________

____

____

____

____

____

____

____

____

____

Journal

Date: ____

I'm grateful for: _________________________________

____

My goal for today is: _____________________________

____

What is on my heart today: _______________________

____

____

____

____

____

____

____

____

____

____

Journal

Date: _______________________________________

I'm grateful for: ____________________________
____

My goal for today is: ________________________
____

What is on my heart today: ___________________
____
____
____
____
____
____
____
____
____

Journal

Date: ____

I'm grateful for: _____________________________________

____

My goal for today is: _________________________________

____

What is on my heart today: ____________________________

____

____

____

____

____

____

____

____

____

Journal

Date: _______________________________________

I'm grateful for: _____________________________

____

My goal for today is: _________________________

____

What is on my heart today: ____________________

____

____

____

____

____

____

____

____

____

Journal

Date: ____

I'm grateful for: ___________________________________
____

My goal for today is: _______________________________
____

What is on my heart today: __________________________

____

____

____

____

____

____

____

____

Journal

Date: ___________________________________

I'm grateful for: _______________________

____

My goal for today is: ___________________

____

What is on my heart today: ______________

____

____

____

____

____

____

____

____

____

Journal

Date: ____

I'm grateful for: ____________________________________

____

My goal for today is: ________________________________

____

What is on my heart today: ___________________________

____

____

____

____

____

____

____

____

Journal

Date: ____

I'm grateful for: ___________________________________

____

My goal for today is: _______________________________

____

What is on my heart today: __________________________

____

____

____

____

____

____

____

____

Journal

Date: _______________________________

I'm grateful for: _______________________

____

My goal for today is: ____________________

____

What is on my heart today: ________________

____

____

____

____

____

____

____

____

Journal

Date: _______________________________

I'm grateful for: ____________________
____

My goal for today is: _________________
____

What is on my heart today: ____________
____
____
____
____
____
____
____
____
____

Journal

Date: _______________________________________

I'm grateful for: _____________________________

____

My goal for today is: _________________________

____

What is on my heart today: ____________________

____

____

____

____

____

____

____

____

____

Journal

Date: _______________________________________

I'm grateful for: _______________________________
____

My goal for today is: ____________________________
____

What is on my heart today: ________________________
____
____
____
____
____
____
____
____
____

Journal

Date: _______________________________________

I'm grateful for: _____________________________
____

My goal for today is: _________________________
____

What is on my heart today: ____________________
____
____
____
____
____
____
____
____
____

Journal

Date: ____

I'm grateful for: ____________________________________

____

My goal for today is: ________________________________

____

What is on my heart today: ___________________________

____

____

____

____

____

____

____

____

____

Journal

Date: ______________________________

I'm grateful for: ______________________

____

My goal for today is: __________________

____

What is on my heart today: _____________

____

____

____

____

____

____

____

____

Journal

Date: ____

I'm grateful for: ______________________________________

____

My goal for today is: __________________________________

____

What is on my heart today: _____________________________

____

____

____

____

____

____

____

____

Journal

Date: ____

I'm grateful for: ____________________________________

____

My goal for today is: ________________________________

____

What is on my heart today: ___________________________

____

____

____

____

____

____

____

____

____

Journal

Date: _______________________________________

I'm grateful for: _____________________________

____

My goal for today is: _________________________

____

What is on my heart today: ____________________

____

____

____

____

____

____

____

____

Journal

Date: ___________________________________

I'm grateful for: _________________________

____

My goal for today is: _____________________

____

What is on my heart today: _______________

____

____

____

____

____

____

____

____

Journal

Date: _______________________________

I'm grateful for: _______________________

____

My goal for today is: ____________________

____

What is on my heart today: _______________

____

____

____

____

____

____

____

____

Journal

Date: _______________________________________

I'm grateful for: ____________________________

____

My goal for today is: ________________________

____

What is on my heart today: ___________________

____

____

____

____

____

____

____

____

____

Journal

Date: ____

I'm grateful for: _____________________________________
____

My goal for today is: _________________________________
____

What is on my heart today: ____________________________
____
____
____
____
____
____
____
____

Journal

Date: _______________________________________

I'm grateful for: ______________________________

____

My goal for today is: ___________________________

____

What is on my heart today: _______________________

____

____

____

____

____

____

____

____

Journal

Date: ____

I'm grateful for: _________________________________

____

My goal for today is: _____________________________

____

What is on my heart today: ________________________

____

____

____

____

____

____

____

____

____

Journal

Date: ____

I'm grateful for: ____________________________________

____

My goal for today is: ________________________________

____

What is on my heart today: __________________________

____

____

____

____

____

____

____

____

Journal

Date: _______________________________________

I'm grateful for: ___________________________
____

My goal for today is: ______________________
____

What is on my heart today: _________________
____
____
____
____
____
____
____
____

Journal

Date: _______________________________________

I'm grateful for: _____________________________

____

My goal for today is: _________________________

____

What is on my heart today: ____________________

____

____

____

____

____

____

____

____

____

Journal

Date: _______________________________________

I'm grateful for: _____________________________

____

My goal for today is: _________________________

____

What is on my heart today: ____________________

____

____

____

____

____

____

____

____

Journal

Date: ____

I'm grateful for: _____________________________________

____

My goal for today is: _________________________________

____

What is on my heart today: ____________________________

____

____

____

____

____

____

____

____

____

Journal

Date: _______________________________________

I'm grateful for: _______________________________

____

My goal for today is: ____________________________

____

What is on my heart today: _______________________

____

____

____

____

____

____

____

____

Journal

Date: ____

I'm grateful for: ________________________________
____

My goal for today is: ____________________________
____

What is on my heart today: _______________________
____
____
____
____
____
____
____
____

Journal

Date: ___________________________________

I'm grateful for: _______________________
____

My goal for today is: ___________________
____

What is on my heart today: ______________
____
____
____
____
____
____
____
____
____

Journal

Date: _________________________________

I'm grateful for: _______________________

____

My goal for today is: ___________________

____

What is on my heart today: ______________

____

____

____

____

____

____

____

____

Journal

Date: ____

I'm grateful for: ___________________________________
____

My goal for today is: _______________________________
____

What is on my heart today: _________________________
____
____
____
____
____
____
____
____
____

Journal

Date: _______________________________

I'm grateful for: _______________________
____

My goal for today is: ____________________
____

What is on my heart today: _______________
____
____
____
____
____
____
____
____
____

Journal

Date: _______________________________

I'm grateful for: _______________________________

____

My goal for today is: _______________________________

____

What is on my heart today: _______________________________

____

____

____

____

____

____

____

____

____

Journal

Date: _________________________________

I'm grateful for: _______________________

____

My goal for today is: ____________________

____

What is on my heart today: _______________

____

____

____

____

____

____

____

____

____

Journal

Date: ____

I'm grateful for: ____________________________________

____

My goal for today is: ________________________________

____

What is on my heart today: ___________________________

____

____

____

____

____

____

____

____

____

Journal

Date: ____

I'm grateful for: ______________________________

____

My goal for today is: __________________________

____

What is on my heart today: ______________________

____

____

____

____

____

____

____

____

____

Journal

Date: _______________________________________

I'm grateful for: ___________________________

____

My goal for today is: _______________________

____

What is on my heart today: __________________

____

____

____

____

____

____

____

____

Journal

Date: ___________________________________

I'm grateful for: _______________________

____

My goal for today is: ___________________

____

What is on my heart today: ______________

____

____

____

____

____

____

____

____

____

Journal

Date: _______________________________________

I'm grateful for: ______________________________

____

My goal for today is: __________________________

____

What is on my heart today: _____________________

____

____

____

____

____

____

____

____

____

Journal

Date: _______________________________________

I'm grateful for: ____________________________

____

My goal for today is: _________________________

____

What is on my heart today: ____________________

____

____

____

____

____

____

____

____

____

Journal

Date: ____

I'm grateful for: _____________________________________

____

My goal for today is: _________________________________

____

What is on my heart today: ____________________________

____

____

____

____

____

____

____

____

____

Journal

Date: _______________________________

I'm grateful for: _____________________

____

My goal for today is: __________________

____

What is on my heart today: ______________

____

____

____

____

____

____

____

____

____

Journal

Date: _______________________________________

I'm grateful for: _____________________________
____

My goal for today is: _________________________
____

What is on my heart today: ____________________
____
____
____
____
____
____
____
____
____

Journal

Date: _______________________________________

I'm grateful for: ___________________________

____

My goal for today is: _______________________

____

What is on my heart today: __________________

____

____

____

____

____

____

____

____

____

Journal

Date: _______________________________

I'm grateful for: _______________________________

____

My goal for today is: _______________________________

____

What is on my heart today: _______________________________

____

____

____

____

____

____

____

____

____

Journal

Date: ____

I'm grateful for: ________________________________

____

My goal for today is: ____________________________

____

What is on my heart today: _______________________

____

____

____

____

____

____

____

____

____

Journal

Date: _______________________________________

I'm grateful for: _____________________________

____

My goal for today is: _________________________

____

What is on my heart today: ____________________

____

____

____

____

____

____

____

____

____

Journal

Date: ____

I'm grateful for: _________________________________

____

My goal for today is: _____________________________

____

What is on my heart today: ________________________

____

____

____

____

____

____

____

____

____

Journal

Date: _______________________________

I'm grateful for: _______________________________

____

My goal for today is: _______________________________

____

What is on my heart today: _______________________________

____

____

____

____

____

____

____

____

____

Journal

Date: ____

I'm grateful for: _________________________________

____

My goal for today is: _____________________________

____

What is on my heart today: ________________________

____

____

____

____

____

____

____

____

Journal

Date: ______________________________________

I'm grateful for: ___________________________

____

My goal for today is: _______________________

____

What is on my heart today: __________________

____

____

____

____

____

____

____

____

____

Journal

Date: ____

I'm grateful for: ___________________________________

____

My goal for today is: _______________________________

____

What is on my heart today: __________________________

____

____

____

____

____

____

____

____

____

Journal

Date: ____

I'm grateful for: ___________________________________

____

My goal for today is: _______________________________

____

What is on my heart today: __________________________

____

____

____

____

____

____

____

____

____

CLOSING PRAYER

Dear Heavenly Father, I ask a special blessing on the person reading this book. Please grant them peace and comfort on the days that are the most difficult, healing for their broken hearts, grace when they fail, and guidance for the long and difficult path ahead. Please, Father, surround them with loving people, and grant them protection from unkindness. I ask, Father, that you put people in their life to uplift them and give them hope and joy again. It is by your hand that they be fully restored. I ask these things in your son's Jesus' name, Amen.

A portion of the proceeds of this book will be donated to the Wounded Warrior Project in memory of my beautiful son, Conrad Lile.

Our grief journey is not meant to be traveled alone. If this journal has touched your life, I would love to hear about it. Or if you would like to connect with me, please send comments to this email: SemperFimom89@gmail.com

www.ingramcontent.com/pod-product-compliance
Lightning Source LLC
Chambersburg PA
CBHW051819150726